Also by Kinereth Gensler
Someone Is Human in THREESOME POEMS

WITHOUT ROOF

Poems by Kinereth Gensler

Alice James Books   Cambridge, Massachusetts

Library of Congress Catalogue Card Number 80-70829
ISBN 0-914086-32-4
Printed in the United States of America

Cover drawing by Shlomith Haber-Schaim

Design by Amanda Freymann
Typesetting by Jeffrey Schwartz
Paste-up by Aspect Composition

Alice James Books are published by the Alice James Poetry
Cooperative, Inc., 138 Mount Auburn Street, Cambridge,
Massachusetts 02138.

The publication of this book was made possible with support from the
Massachusetts Council on the Arts and Humanities, a state agency whose
funds are recommended by the Governor and appropriated by the
Legislature.

I would like to thank the editors of the following publications, in which versions of these poems originally appeared:

Blacksmith Anthology, Choomia, Green House, Lynx, Massachusetts Review, Midstream, New Orlando Poetry Anthology, Ploughshares, Prairie Schooner, Radcliffe Quarterly, Real Paper, Shenandoah, Stonecloud, Virginia Quarterly Review, Woman Poet, Women/Poems, Word Guild Magazine.

The following poems are reprinted from the section entitled *Someone Is Human* in THREESOME POEMS published by Alice James Books in 1976:

"The Air in This Room," "Dandelions," "The Fabulous, The Extinct and the Real," "Fog Poem," "From the Residue of Mythologies," "Jerusalem of Stone," "In Time" and "Sestina: An Old Story."

CONTENTS

III TRAVELLING BACKWARDS

In memory of my parents, Alexander and Julia Dushkin

I The Border

Field Exercise

You're picking wildflowers in a minefield:

Spread yourself out.
The weight of a body spread-eagled
is safest.
Inch through the dangerous grass
as you would over quicksand.

Such huge anemones! pink,
lavender, the brightest scarlet.
You come through barbed wire,
past signs that say *Keep to the Road,*
This Area Not Cleared of Land Mines.
You could blow yourself up.
You could be arrested.

This is always the border,
this abundance.
You have the whole field to yourself,
as if there were no end to wildflowers
and anyone
could freely fill her arms with flowers.

When picking wildflowers in a minefield,
slide your fingers down each stem.
Snap carefully.
Don't tug at the roots.

Cave

Old tenants sleep here.
In the hooked darkness
we stumble through droppings—
the bat smell sifts down on us,
holes fall away from the floor,
hole inside hole, no footing.

Cave fever! Bat-bite!

What was it we had climbed to
in the sunshine
across fields of stone,
was it the concept, *cave*,
defensible, prehistoric?

I remember an overhang of rock,
shadows beneath it,
something light, something green.

The cave's mouth fooled us
with its clusters of cyclamen leaves
and white winter crocus.
We were looking for shade—
not this cold, rabid place,
a hole to crawl from.

I remember the bright threshold.

We were climbing.

We were looking for wildflowers.

Sestina: An Old Story

The child had 20-20 vision.
The clue was always there: that episode
where she picks wildflowers in the wood,
when, basket on her arm, she meets the wolf
and still won't hurry, still can't keep her eyes
from thickets where blue hyacinths lie hidden.

We see her next at the door, half-hidden
by flowers, basket, hood—a vision
from our first picturebooks. She is all eyes,
all innocence, a pawn in episodes
whose end is preordained: the wolf
is slain; she learns to fear the wood.

"Come in, my dear!" he cries, as we knew he would.
He's tucked in bed, his whiskers hidden
by Grandmother's nightcap, but he looks like a wolf.
Could any child, with even partial vision,
be fooled by such a flimsy episode?
Some secret lay behind that snout, those eyes,

some great unfolding. With her own eyes
she'd seen those wondrous changes in the wood,
watching a stone move (cautious, its head hidden),
watching the leaf with wings, the snake's episode
of shed skin. Do people undergo revision?
Old people? Grandmother? Is she this wolf?

Now (in that queer, high-pitched voice), the wolf:
"Come closer, child!"—"But, Grandmother, what big eyes
you've got!" (What ears! What teeth!)—Could she envision
herself transformed, made meek, incurious, or would
she wait to learn the secret hidden
from children until the final episode?

The hunter dominates that episode.
He does not hear her cries, he hears the wolf's
loud snoring. And she, swallowed alive, hidden
in that dark gut, sees through corrected eyes
how wrong it is to dawdle in the wood,
how dangerous to trust her small girl's vision.

She learns: meet each new episode with downcast eyes.
Avoid: wolf, flowers, turtle, butterfly, snake, wood.
Be good. Be safe. Stay hidden. Abandon vision.

Jerusalem of Stone

I

You could be blind here.
Among the rough stone walls
and the smooth dressed faces of houses
you could be Isaac,
taking your cue from stone.
The voices of Jacob and Esau

call from opposing rooftops.
You stand at the Western Wall,
separate, a woman
torn between rams' horns
and the minaret's loud speakers.
You touch the stones. You listen.

In this city of many layers,
where each new war
uncovers earlier stonework
and the steps go down to bedrock,
the sun still walks on the walls
and the tower of David.

Late in the afternoon,
when he walks on his rooftop,
you could, without loss, be a stone,
unquestioning in the light,
washed in its radiance only,
blind as Bathsheba bathing.

II

What I know of stone:

how it is sun
after the sun goes down

how cold overcomes it
and it contracts
holding the crease of light
for eons if need be

how far quakes reach it
tremors running
beneath the sea and mountains
the pressure of trapped suns
building inside it and the shrug
the long and patient stone-shrug

how it shakes free and waits
crack by hairline crack
till blown seeds find it
anemone cyclamen me
held fast by this stone
flowering holding it

The Border

*The war broke out in autumn at the empty border
between sweet grapes and oranges.* —Yehuda Amichai

War or peace, the border is never empty,
growing its wildflowers and weeds,
making the most of a difficult position.

And the cash crops aren't meant for your table.
You're an old hand dragging that wagon to market:
grapes, oranges, wheat

whatever the harvest, it's earmarked for export.
You ship it abroad, make do
with dandelion greens and milkweed.

When war breaks out,
weeds will sustain you.
You rely on chicory.
And the Good Soldier Thistle. . .

This story belonged to your mother,
it's the one she loved telling:

At nightfall, after the first World War, in those
months of upheaval, stranded in a broken-down car in
the hills of Judea, afraid of the isolate terrain, afraid
of the driver, she saw from the road's edge a blue flower,
followed it into a stony field, and picked it.

In the fading light it was a beacon, blue as amulets
are blue. Reaching through thorns, her fingers uncovered
a box and wires, and a voice came to her out of the
ground: *What number are you calling? May I help you?*

After a time she answered, forcing herself to speak
into a field telephone, left over from the war, still
connected. She told what landmarks she had seen, where
she had come from and where she was headed.

And rescue came. They lifted the car and driver
into a huge lorry, scooping her up, taking her straight
to her destination!

From her fear, a woman makes a story
and tells it to her daughters.
Telling it, she names it:
The Blue Thistle.

In the blue blaze of thorn along the border,
in the desolate spaces,
a real voice speaks from the ground,
a weed called by its name becomes a flower.

Something brave is growing.

Dandelions

Old woman
muttering up the road,
in queer shoes striding
along the highway with no sidewalks,
in a man's old felt hat
bending to pick unkempt grasses,
filling your market basket
at the edges where the power-mower
and the scythers cannot reach,
where the golf-course and the graveyard fences stop,
where unstunted dandelions, growing fiercely,
are greens for your dinner
and fat blond heads for your winter wine—

driving that road
I see you move into my line of vision,
walking the highway's fringe,
defiant, picking.
I slow to pass—
you flicker at the rolled-down window:
the felt hat slips,
the gray fuzz on your head blows toward me, reaching.
I shiver in the bright June morning.

Our faces meet inside my rear-view mirror,
sister, June's indestructible blown weed.

Inside

No ideas but an itch.
I scratch it, it hums,
it's humming now,
a green dew is gathering.

If I smoke it out
will it burn off in sunlight,
slightly fizzy,
hissing like applewood?
Or will it thicken?

Perhaps it will become
the glorious confirmation of
my reality as a green creature:
by day, a hummingbird,
by night, a cricket.

What do I know about crickets?
They make a compulsive sound, a thin drumming,
like an itch.
All summer long, all night,
they keep it up outside my window.

Right now it's winter.
In winter I wait for green,
that cricket sound by which, in the dark,
I recognize summer.

The Fabulous, The Extinct and the Real

Under the snow—in China, perhaps,
or Egypt, or the Mesozoic—
the birds gone from our skies
are wintering. Is it the Everglades
they nest in? Does Scheherazade
see them from her window?
I speak of them all: rocs,
pterodactyls and passenger pigeons
as well as storks and robins.
In this season, each
is as much gone as the others.

Somewhere it is spring: the times
and families of earth hold reunion. There,
where the globe splits along its seam,
a profusion of the possible occurs—
a continuum of wings.
I expect a messenger at any moment.
Tugging at worms, he will uncover
the crack in my garden.

To a Pragmatist

Poetry, you said (not sure
it was good or bad) could be
about anything at all,
like a doorknob, for instance—
but *you*, you said, would make it
a celestial doorknob.

So I brought you this doorknob,
a bright, ceramic knob made
in the Old City. It shows
a white dove on a green field
surrounded by blue flowers.

Touché, you said, but no thanks,
it's too large, too unwieldy,
too ornate, the shaft's too long,
it would never fit the door.

Take it anyway, will you?
Use it as a paperweight
or weapon. At least, save it.
Keep this doorknob-shaped object
for whatever it opens.

The Air in This Room

The children lift from their desks.
They glide to the chalkboard, buzzing.
Paintings are hung there: dreamings. Chalk dust
shimmers in sunlight.

The children hover. Their hands
dip over pencils. They dart like fish,
like dragonflies, the strange bright birds
they make poems from.

The air in this room is older than oceans.
Turned to the sun, the first plants breathed it.
Light seeped inward. The color of dreams
entered their leaves.

The Wind Harp

They say there's a vast harp
set on a hill
the wind playing through it
spring summer autumn winter
the wind moving
through giant harpstrings
tying the earth and sky together
and worshippers come
whole churchfuls listening
to the music of the spheres
the picnics! the grass blowing!

I think of the harp being built
a year and a half in creation
and the man who built it
a craftsman
waiting to hear the wind move
through a thing of his own making
I think of how he moved on
leaving his harp to the weather

How to Water the Flowers

Before dawn, the sound of pumps:
water rising into rooftop tanks.
The rainy season has passed—

one tank is your week's ration.
Drain it off while it's coming!
Fill every container in the house:

pots, kettles, buckets,
pitchers, basins, sinks,
fill scrub pails, and then

while it is dark
and the tank is still filling,
plug the tub. Stand

under pouring water. Let it rise
to the brim, till all the members
of your household have showered.

In this saved and soapy water,
wash the clothes—
the whole week's laundry.

Next, bail out the tub.
With this tubwater
you may wash the floor.

Put your wetmop through the wringer,
filling a bucket with wrung-out,
used-three-times-over, water.

This water is yours, it is free.
Now water the flowers in the garden—
some will survive.

II   Without Roof

Leaving the Thruway

So, imperceptibly, we come to the end of loving
as to the abrupt edge of a highway under construction,
its funds cut off by a bankrupt state.
Born to the freeway and the four-leaf clover,
we have no skills to take us past this place.

The whole world shifts: no riders here, no drivers.
In the chill dawn at the checkpoint of the desert
we leave the car and make our way through sand.
And love, the junction of the green horizon,
becomes again one woman and one man.

The Exile

Where the hot sands blow
the heart is a cool place, and leafy.
It wraps a tenderness and keeps it moist.
But we have come to winter's island—
the grape vines are bare,
no figs or date palms grow,
and I have cut my hair.

A Game of Solitaire

Seagreen formica,
the seven stacks of cards
laid out like footprints
hardening in the sand.

The sea moves.
It makes random erasures.

You move a card. You wait
for undertows and holes,
obliterations for a king to fill.
You wait alone,
safe on a low tide beach.
No buddy check.
Cheating, you cannot drown.

The game's called Patience.

Cards slip through your hands like beads,
like butts,
like empty beercans littering the beach.
What good is it, lady?
The most you'll win,
stacked on the green table,
is four, flat-faced kings.

At the highwater line you dream
some gift from the sea.
You pray for luck—
the overwhelming tide, a clean sweep.

A Woman Watching

Two white ducks at nightfall
coming my way
dazzling as spotlights
their pale, broad bills
dipping, fishing
beneath black lily pads.

The old hypnosis. Light,
the brightness—
white nibs on the dark stream
probing, going under.

Eclipsed in that blinding
charcoal shadows
detach themselves slowly:
duck-shapes vague
as shrugged dreams,
as dark spots swimming
before the eyes.

> At the stream's edge, waiting
> for you as always,
> I watch them move into
> a kind of focus:

> three shadowed ducks,
> faintly mottled,
> moving in convoy
> with two white drakes.

> Hardly a target.
> For a woman watching,
> more like thunder.
> Mates. The egg-layers.

After Eden

something got named
which had been nameless,
Apple:

Eve's fruit-guilt.
The bulge in Adam's craw
too thick to swallow.

Before, in the garden,
trees were anonymous: "good-to-eat,"
"pleasant-to-look-at."

Adam gave names
only to creatures: the beasts,
birds, cattle

and his wife, Eve.

Something red
got fingered after Eden
which in her hand

had been dark fruit,
plucked from the tree, "Knowledge-
of-good-and-evil."

Men could choke
on so vague a clue. Was it fig,
apricot, pomegranate?

A is for Apple,
the smooth, round fruit
branded scarlet.

Quake

A cool September evening and a hearth.
We piled up logs and kindling, watched them flare
—the chimney shook: a sootblack bird
broke through the flames and heaved across the room,
crashing its beak against the window glass,
beating the room to blackness with singed wings
until the shades were drawn,
a door thrown open,
and it disappeared. . .

As if—in strict reversal of the spheres—
a man were falling through an eagles' world:
some huge, red mammal from a burning plane
who, with fingers scraping against a crag,
jars their high nest. As if, uncaring,
he drops from sight—and leaves behind
a scattering of eggs,
scorched twigs,
and two stunned, flightless birds.

Past Bearing

A baby cries: I stiffen—
still, with dry breasts,
that long, sweet tug returns.

In Sparta it was quicker.
Exposed, placed on a hillside
far beyond the city,

a woman in her withering
heard only the vulture's cry.

Gathering Place

In the standstill of time she is rocking,
    in the least place for journeys,
    moving nowhere but moving
    inside an old containment.
    Something of weight is recalled
    at her shoulder and in her
    lap, quiet, the rhythmical
    bedsprings. She is pushing off
    to the playground with her feet,
    swinging up on her bike.

She rocks in the fullness of scarred maple,
    at ease in the upper berth,
    complete, green-curtained, her shoes
    tucked into the side hammock
    and the train hooting, the ship's
    engines churning beneath her
    and the jets straining against
    her center at take-off.

She is not rocking backwards or forwards
    but gathering inside her,
    knowing the chair will tell her
    when to get off and where.

The Music Buff

keeps tuning the dial to find it,
has to keep tuning, deaf
to what breaks in: the news,
snow cancellations, the station
announcing its own existence.

You have to want it a lot,
loud and pure and always,
to fiddle like this while the world
burns on its axis.

And what if the tubes
blow out, or you're stuck somewhere
with only a handful of stations,
none of them music, real music?

The walls are thin. You're caught
in the storm's eye, listening
to the moaning next door,
the click,
and your own heart beating.

Because Our Eyes Are Changing

because we can no longer read
the fine print
or lift the heavy news-
paper at the door

because the screen is blurred
whirling with snow
sunspots   blood   all seasons
equalized by the camera

only what's far is clear
seen from the moon
the earth's blue curve
and all its fullness

the world distorts
turns flat
upon reentry

needing to hold ourselves
at arm's length
from that flattening

we read
the braille dots
rising on our skins

Of Lemmings, Those Strong Swimmers

They think that the ocean
is one more river.
On its far bank, beyond the horizon,
shoots of dwarf birch are waiting—
moss! grass! reindeer lichen!

They think—the collective mousebrain thinks:
I ford the streams, I can swim
the breadth of a moat, I float
with the current of rivers,
I have crossed them all, I can make it.

O brave, insatiable lemmings,
prodigious in the tunnels,
in the long Scandinavian nights breeding,
who in your hunger
strip the tundra,

who strip the highlands, lowlands,
coastal cities,
who gnaw the rigging off ships,
you of the thin, furred bodies
swimming toward us:

the ocean is vast,
only its vastness saves us.
Huddled on this far shore
we salute
your fortuitous drowning.

Fork

Late autumn. Birds branch on the sky,
trunks of bare trees move upward,
splintered and black,
like ice-cracks on the river.

Yellow is gone from the yellow wood—
that divergence of roads
seen clearly in the stripped air.

We reach the fork. It points itself
like a pronged stick dowsing,
hovering over frozen ground.

Stiff-legged on the ice, we run
together, apart—old sled dogs
held by an ancient leash.

You follow the sun.
I follow the line of myself outward
into the first cracking-place,
a deep strain.

You disappear.

I follow the trace of running water.

Without Roof

The finger beckons.
A thin bridge stretches across the gorge,
a vine, or tightrope.
You with your fear of falling are unable
to use it, but the finger
—white gloved, stylized, a mime's—
beckons.

You think of those New Hampshire covered bridges,
the old survivors,
where they'd bring snow in
for sleighs to pass over more easily.

What will be brought for you?

Here is the foot bridge:
open-sided rails,
spaces between the planks.
Underneath—the long drop over rocks—
white water is rushing.
Without roof, the wind whistles and you sway
in the sky's vertigo.

Your task is to cross the gorge,
to finish the crossing.
Not to be frozen at midpoint
so that ever after they say,

She gets halfway across a bridge
and turns back.

Is it the mocking of that voice which drives you
or the insistent gesture of the mime?

Under some truce, a compromise of sky,
you lean into the wind,
a slanted upright
moving forward in fear
from high place to high place.

III   Travelling Backwards

It Happens in a Foreign Country

that is more like home than home   pygmy goats
appear among rocks across the wadi   they are nibbling
invisible tufts of grass   their backs are to you
they recede   climbing   into the basalt hills
this is not an oasis   the road   made discontinuous
by flashfloods keeps happening
is bridged   falters

                              this is not a mirage   it is where
                         around each bend in the salt desert
                      hanging from isolate squat trees you see
                          those dark inviolable cloth bundles
      the spare possessions of a nomad   wrapped in a cloak
                         tied to a tamarisk tree and left there
                            for weeks   months   whole seasons
                            to be lived without   but saved
                                     to be returned to

if you leave the bus now it will happen
among red rocks   porphyry   Nubian sandstone
you will recognize the tree   discover
what it was   so carefully wrapped   you had put away
long years ago   before your travels
they will all be dry now   those belongings
perhaps you meant to save the cloak
in the desert   you will need a cloak

travelling backwards

because someone has died
flying into dawn
lifting off year after year
through fog & sunhatch
no one is left who says *See
how beautiful it all is darling*
on the plane waiting you see
daybreak a scar
how the torn sky whitens
and how the Matterhorn
shaped after all like an alp
is nobody's mother

At Such Times of Divestiture

for Jeannine

Our mothers are gone, they're gone and we are full-
grown now, we don't need them. Their deaths
leave no hole that won't fill at the graveside.

Men, at such times of divestiture, take on
the persona of animals, they move swiftly to become
the great-beaked birds: herons, kingfishers.

Our training is otherwise. Heavy-bottomed and weighted
we sit in dirt, legs outstretched, our hair thrown forward.
Immobile, we move slightly, hugging ourselves.

It is a way of being while the sun beats on our shoulders.
We are famous for being women. Like stones,
like our mothers before us, we warm from the top downwards.

She never cried, that I can remember. This dry weeping
waters the earth. Will we crumble?
Will our hair take root in this spot,
will we utterly replace them?

Closed Poem

I make a cluster
of words around her
oh mother! I say don't!
no! never! and they hang there
in the space
where words hang
all that hot air encased
in bright round colors
well I'm sorry! I say
which has always enraged her

She will rip
the ends of the strings
out of my hand
the words will snag on nails
they will catch on thorns
stop! I say
but she's dead   shrunken
all those balloons   that bright
irretrievable color

Poem in a Time of Chrysanthemums

Where are the boundaries?

In the orange light, sparrows are gathering,
their small voices charge the air.
Will they too migrate, these homebirds,
bereaving the landscape?

Fire halo,
light from the mountain ash, bright berries,
burns down to lava.

Yes they will migrate, beyond the volcano,
they will fall
past the scalding lip into
a new generation.

To empty, to turn.

Sweet fruit in my hands,
the sound of sparrows.

Annuals

That color has gone   all of it
all of that purple is
        finally
                missing
it was your color

I follow it on the street
finger it on the dress racks
and now the garden
these deep velvets
        petunias
                pansies
I have to keep planting them

even your amethyst brooch has gone
there where you are
        among pale blues
                vinca and rosemary
layers of stone

Learning, With Archeologists

The curved fragment lies
among shards and wild crocus,
an artifact unearthed
near the stopped road.
Bulldozers are idling in the sun.

Identify, he says. We have come
across fields marked with flags
to the place where archeologists
do their slow dance on rubble,
up the sliced hill,
coins of Antiochus IV warming their pockets.

Jug, he says, *Part of the Lip.*
He restores antiquities,
assembling pieces.
The village elders wait
for this process, History, to be over
so the road can continue.

As for me, I know that history is private.
The uncovered bones of my mother
will tell nothing
of the words that came
springing from her lip,
their shimmer. Or how
a woman blurs,
becomes absorbed, becomes landscape.

The Pompeii Exhibit

Skeletons belong to a race of bones
whose name
is Skeleton

they are not real
nothing replaces
the flesh

we walk past statues
wild boar and snapping dogs
the marble goddess Aphrodite

how shall we know those lost people

we walk on the edge
between Pompeii and mist

       *   *   *

Here is a city drowned by lava
it could be our city
no one is ready
we are caught in the act
decadent   hopeful

here they are equal
patricians and slaves
having just drawn the bath water

fumes engulf them
hot ash sifts over them
then the cooling   the hardening

under volcanic ash
a body dwindles

it becomes contour
a shaped hollow

      *   *   *

This sprawled girl is why we keep coming

wet plaster filled
the cavity
that was her body

face down   arm at her forehead
the abandoned legs
the half-clothed torso

like Danish bog people
and mastodons under ice
she is encased forever in her flesh

we too may be found that way
caught unawares
as if playing statues

From the Residue of Mythologies

There is always a goat-herd,
a wet nurse, a simple woodman,
someone nameless
who saves the baby.

Always someone, ignorant
or defiant of orders,
who unbinds the child's ankles
or lifts him from the bulrushes.

Someone thwarts the king.
Someone is human.

Even now, on a pocked road
under exploding fires
a child is being snatched
from the sky's betrayal.

And later, in another
part of the forest,
someone will be left
who saves the baby,

if only a lonely she-wolf,
suckling the last, small man-things.

Fog Poem

This or that, says the mind:
mountains, or the ocean;

a climate for lemons
or a climate for apples.

I

You come to the Bay
(chance takes you
or you're born there
like any stranger),
you come to a steep house near the ocean.
In front, there's a lemon tree;
in back, an apple.
Your windows face the great suspension bridges.
The weather is fog.

Fog is the sign of the Bay,
its first condition,
suspending the view for hours,
suspending vision,
condensing in fine, cool particles of water
on fruit trees and the bells of fuchsias,
bathing the small leaves of live oaks, entering
the fire-resistant core of redwoods.

You wait for the fog to lift
each day, unfailing;
the warmth on your skin, the sun
filling the air with bridges.

II

The Bay is elsewhere.
A hole in the mind remains,
an absence

where a tooth was.
Fog drifts
over the same old narrows,

under the isolated tips of towers.
It goes round and round.
It bangs its head against abutments.

You feel for the hole.
You reach behind it.
In the lurch of time and space

a real fog answers.
It lifts as it comes, it clears.
You touch the roadway.

Sangam of the Cauvery River, Mysore

At the fork where rivers meet,
the confluence, *sangam*,
is holy.

Broad stone steps go down to the river,
each step a landing.

A woman washes her sari.
A man and his child wade to the grassy island.

Ashes of the dead flow by me.
If I give the river a coin
it will say a prayer in its flowing

for those who have died this year:
Alex, my father.
Julia, my mother.

Every week of their life he brought her flowers.

At this sangam,
where the branching river
meets itself again,

I place my offering on the waters:
garland of roses and jasmine,
these braided flowers.

The Traveller and the Elephant

Kaziranga, North India

riding the elephant sideways
in a gray flannel skirt
camouflaged
she approaches wild rhinos

        bare feet of the driver
        steer the elephant's ears
        three meters off the ground
        her own feet dangling
        she grips the handrails

                nothing prepared her
                for the mounting
                stairs and platform
                the launching tower

she remembers ivory
the elephants' graveyard
in an old Tarzan film
and now this elephant a detusked male
moving at daybreak toward the river

                she wears the long gray skirt
                with its faint smell of elephant
                to symphony
                fanfare of trumpets
                oh marvelous the blind violinist

not that she can't comprehend the elephant
or adapt to its motion
a slow roll
like a mild turbulence of ocean
in which she is not seasick

but that she never knew this kind of transport
plodding through marshland
half grass half water
trusting the great feet far beneath her
the coarse reeds opening before her

Destination

I arrive at the animals reluctant
to use them
we ourselves should be enough
the stories are about us
as for birds they've always stood for
the unknowable verbs
as for grass grain flowers that shake the earth
with small unstoppable explosions
as for bonsai trees and redwoods
the extremes of butterfly and rock
as for grasshopper and ant
grapes and the fox
all Aesop's fables
those creatures that stand for us
stand also for themselves
as you and I stand also for ourselves
nobody's animals

In Time

If she could be their storyteller.

Or if from mustard seeds
and wool-gathering she
could weave them bright blankets.

To be that Roman whose stone bridge
two thousand years
still spans the Tagus River!
Or be that bridge.

She is instead a hostelry.

Knapsacks appeal at her fire,
moments of singing.
Her rug is worn through near the firescreen
and her rooms breathe road dust.
They come and go.

O someday she will have
the youngest and most constant of
her heart's desires.

To be an old
and marvelous woman.

7746